Japan

For a free color catalog describing Gareth Stevens' list of high-quality children's books, call 1-800-341-3569 (USA) or 1-800-461-9120 (Canada).

For their help in the preparation of *Children of the World: Japan*, the editors gratefully thank Ms. Toshiko Takahara, Japan Information Center, New York, NY; Employment and Immigration Canada, Ottawa, Ont.; the US Immigration and Naturalization Service, Washington, DC; the United States Bureau of Public Affairs, Office of Public Communication, Washington, DC, for unencumbered use of material in the public domain; and Jun Amano of Milwaukee, Wisconsin.

Library of Congress Cataloging-in-Publication Data

Birmingham, Lucy, 1956-
    Japan / photography by Lucy Birmingham; edited by Meredith Ackley, Susan Taylor-Boyd, Rhoda Irene Sherwood. — North American ed.
       p. cm. — (Children of the world)
    "First and originally published by Kaisei-sha Publishing Co., Ltd., Tokyo"—Pref.
    "This work was originally published in shortened form consisting of section 1 only. Photographs and text by Lucy Birmingham"—Pref.
    Bibliography: p.
    Includes index.
    Summary: Text and photographs present the lives of two children in Tokyo and a reference section presents Japan's history, geography, culture, industry, and natural resources.
    ISBN 0-8368-0121-0
    1. Japan—Social life and customs—1945- —Juvenile literature. 2. Children—Japan—Juvenile literature. [1. Japan—Social life and customs.] I. Ackley, Meredith. II. Taylor-Boyd, Susan, 1949- III. Sherwood, Rhoda. IV. Title. V. Series: Children of the world (Milwaukee, Wis.)
DS822.5.B57 1989   952—dc20   89-11493

North American edition first published in 1990 by

Gareth Stevens Children's Books
RiverCenter Building, Suite 201
1555 North RiverCenter Drive
Milwaukee, Wisconsin 53212, USA

Series editor: Rhoda Irene Sherwood
Research editor: Scott Enk
Map design: Sheri Gibbs

Printed in the United States of America

2 3 4 5 6 7 8 9 96 95 94 93 92 91 90

Children of the World

Japan

By Lucy Birmingham

Edited by Meredith Ackley,
Susan Taylor-Boyd, and
Rhoda Irene Sherwood

Gareth Stevens Publishing

MILWAUKEE

. . . a note about *Children of the World*:

The children of the world live in fishing towns, Arctic regions, and urban centers, on islands and in mountain valleys, on sheep ranches and fruit farms. This series follows one child in each country through the pattern of his or her life. Candid photographs show the children with their families, at school, at play, and in their communities. The text describes the dreams of the children and, often through their own words, tells how they see themselves and their lives.

Each book also explores events that are unique to the country in which the child lives, including festivals, religious ceremonies, and national holidays. The *Children of the World* series does more than tell about foreign countries. It introduces children of each country and shows readers what it is like to be a child in that country.

. . . and about *Japan*:

Masayo Funato and her brother Hirofumi live in Tokyo with their parents and grand-parents. Masayo calls her 12-year-old brother a "computer nut" because when he isn't playing with computer games, he's shopping for new ones. Ten-year-old Masayo, who is rather shy, prefers to read and to have her best friend come over to play.

To enhance this book's value in libraries and classrooms, comprehensive reference sections include up-to-date information about Japan's geography, demographics, language, currency, education, culture, industry, and natural resources. *Japan* also features a bibliography, research topics, activity projects, and discussions of such subjects as Tokyo, the country's history, political system, language, and ethnic and religious composition.

The living conditions and experiences of children in Japan vary tremendously according to economic, environmental, and ethnic circumstances. The reference sections help bring to life for young readers the richness and complexity of the culture and heritage of Japan, the events occurring in the nation before and after World War II, and the remarkable growth of its industry in recent years. Of particular interest are discussions of Japan's place in the history of the Far East and its role as a leader in the development of modern technology.

CONTENTS

Masayo and Hirofumi with mother, Kayoko; grandfather, Ryozo; grandmother, Masako; and father, Yoshindo.

LIVING IN JAPAN:
Sister and Brother in a Busy Family

Masayo, 10, and her brother Hirofumi, 12, live with their parents and grandparents in a section of Tokyo called Nerima. In Japan, children, parents, and grandparents often live together. Masayo and Hirofumi often see their other set of grandparents, the Tanakas, who live nearby.

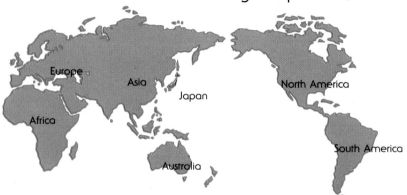

Europe
Asia
Japan
North America
Africa
South America
Australia

Nippon (Japan)

USSR
China
China
Sea of Japan
Tokyo
China Sea
Pacific Ocean

Japan has many people and little land, so people share space. One way they share is to live together. Families also share because keeping the family together is important. Elders are respected.

The Japanese have words that they add to each other's last name to show respect. For instance, the children's mother would not be called by her first name, except by very close friends. Instead, she would be called Funato-san. When she was a young child, Masayo was probably called Masayo-chan. Hirofumi was called Hirofumi-chan or Hirofumi-kun, another choice for boys. After grade school, they too would be called Funato-san.

Another tradition the Funatos still maintain is covering the floors with *tatami* mats. These delicate mats are made of grasses. To protect them and keep them clean, people take off their shoes when entering the house. At one time, people slept on the tatami mats. In some ways, Hirofumi and Masayo's parents and grandparents still prefer them.

Masayo puts her shoes on in the entryway, or *genkan*, of her house.

Traditional sandals mix with more modern shoes outside the door.

Masayo juggles beanbags called *otedama*.

Comic books, or *manga*, waiting to be read.

A Place to Play and Read

Lucky Masayo has her own room. On her shelves are special treasures from places she has visited. Although friends come over to play, Masayo especially likes to read quietly in bed or at her desk. A current favorite is *The Glass Mask*, a comic book about an adventurous actress. Masayo likes this character for she is shy but strong — a bit like Masayo.

Masayo likes to read every chance she gets.

Carefully arranged treasures from trips and friends.

Hirofumi spends most of his free time at the computer.

In Hirofumi's room is his favorite way to kill time — his computer. Masayo says her brother is a computer nut. She teases him because he spends hours playing computer games, alone or with friends. On his bookshelf is a traditional warrior's helmet called a *kabuto.* This is given to boys as a symbol of endurance and strength.

An organized desk.

The kabuto inspires Hirofumi to keep working.

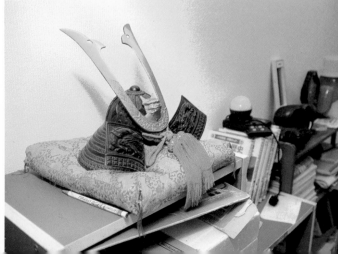

Shopping in Ikebukuro

Today Hirofumi and Masayo go shopping with their parents. It is Hirofumi's birthday, and he gets to pick out his gift. You can guess what he wants! Yes, a computer game.

Usually their mother shops in their neighborhood. But for such a special occasion the family travels downtown to Ikebukuro, one of the main shopping areas of Tokyo.

Japanese people often use public transportation to get around because streets are crowded. Japan imports all of its oil too, which is expensive. So Japanese engineers have designed cars that are small and use little fuel. But because they are costly, many people don't own them. Instead they use trains that travel swiftly within and between cities. The Nerima train station is a five-minute walk from Hirofumi and Masayo's house, so it's easy to get downtown by train. In a few minutes they are in the center of Ikebukuro.

Walking through Nerima to the train station.

Japanese train platforms are large and clean.

The train is modern and fast. But it's also often crowded. At rush hour, these cars are jammed with people.

Wide sidewalks make window-shopping easy.

Examining the choices in a computer shop.

Sunday is a favorite day for the Japanese to shop. Some of the stores are large department stores that carry all kinds of products. But many stores are small — just stalls on the street. The shopkeepers set their products out in baskets on tables. This makes Ikebukuro very colorful and loud. Shop-keepers call to the passers-by that their products are the best and the cheapest.

Hirofumi and Masayo can't help stopping at all the stands to look at everything. Hirofumi stops at the computer stands. But Father suggests they visit a department store where Hirofumi can test out some of the games before he chooses one. Masayo just likes to see the colors and hear vendors shouting at the people to stop. She gives shopkeepers a shy smile when they call to her.

11

Hirofumi tests out a computer game.

Masayo loves toy displays in department stores.

Because this is a special day, Masayo also gets to choose a gift. And Mother has decided they should look for new shoes for the children. Their shoes seem to become too small overnight. Masayo loves to choose new clothes and has quite a flair for fashion.

But with so many choices it's difficult to decide. Finally, she picks out a pair of bright red tennis shoes. She also chooses doll furniture. Now she wants to hurry home to show everything to her best friend, Yumi.

Hirofumi doesn't want to be bothered with shoes. He's having a hard time picking out a game because there are so many challenging ones. He tries out a few — unfortunately, they're all fun, so he wants them all. But at last he chooses a game called "Hero of the Coat of Arms." Now he too wants to hurry home and tell his friends to come over. None of his friends has this game yet, and he wants to show them how to play it.

So many choices — and just in tennis shoes.

They decide to go sightseeing since they are downtown. Nearby is the Sunshine 60 building, the tallest in Tokyo and site of the world's fastest elevator.

Tokyo is so large that you could go by train in one direction for an hour and still be inside the city. But it is not just one big mass. It is many towns clustered together. In fact, that's how the city came to be. Once it was many villages that just grew to form the city we know today.

Ice cream — a treat for everyone.

From the top of the Sunshine 60 building, the family sees Mount Fuji — the tallest and most famous mountain in Japan and a symbol of strength and beauty. They also see an area called Shinjuku, the largest area of Tokyo. Its tall skyscrapers rise into the sky. In the distance, they spot Tokyo's harbor, where ships from all over the world bring raw materials for Japan's industries. After such a busy day, Hirofumi and Masayo ask their parents if they can stop at a teahouse, or *kissaten*. Of course, they want to order ice cream, not tea. Their parents agree — if they can have a few bites.

The city of Tokyo, with Mount Fuji and the Shinjuku district in the distance.

Masayo and Hirofumi enjoy a snack after school.

The Japanese Home

The Funatos' dining room table is very low, and there are no chairs. Instead, everyone sits on cushions and their legs hang down into a space cut out into the floor under the table. Sometimes Hirofumi and Masayo use chopsticks, the traditional Japanese eating utensils. But they also use spoons, knives, and forks for some foods.

Mother and Grandmother prepare traditional Japanese foods like *tempura*. This is a mixture of squid, fish roll, sweet potatoes, carrots, and other vegetables fried in oil. They also make some Western-style foods like fried chicken. Spaghetti is Masayo's favorite food. Almost every day, the family eats rice, a traditional food grown in Japan.

Hirofumi and Masayo bathe almost every night. In Japan, the whole room is a bath and has a drain in the floor. People soap and shampoo themselves outside the tub, using buckets and a hand-held shower. Then they step into hot bathwater for a nice, long soak. The whole family uses the same tub water, so it's important to be rinsed well before soaking.

Naturally, Masayo is shy, photographed in the tub

Most people bathe at home, but some neighborhoods still have the old-style public bath called *sento*, where men and women bathe separately. It costs about 150 yen (around $1.00) to use the sento.

Hirofumi and Masayo's parents and grandparents like to roll out their beds at night onto the tatami mats. Their beds, now popular in the West, are called futons. A futon is a plush pad covered with a cozy comforter. The children think it's too much trouble to roll up the beds each morning and roll them out each night, so they sleep in Western-style beds. Still, they have to tuck in the sheets and covers on these each morning.

Masayo and Yumi playing with dolls.

Masayo takes a nap on her parents' futon.

The principal, Kondo-sensei, talks to the entire school each morning.

Learning at School

Masayo and Hirofumi are busy with school and studies. They attend school six days a week, as most elementary students do in Japan. They go Monday through Saturday, but Saturday is a half day. Students wear uniforms in private schools. Hirofumi and Masayo's uniform is a yellow hat. Other schools have more formal uniforms.

Students begin each day with an 8:30 a.m. assembly in the schoolyard. They organize by class and form neat lines according to height. On Monday the principal gives a pep talk, encouraging everyone to work hard. Other days the children sing or exercise. They call their principal Kondo-sensei. *Sensei*, which means "teacher," is a term of respect.

Today is picture day. Masayo and her friends show off their pictures of fire trucks and ambulances.

Elementary students carry traditional leather book bags — black for boys and red for girls. It's like a backpack and is often quite heavy. Students take most of their books and writing materials home with them every day.

There are five study periods of 45 minutes each and a sixth period for meetings and activities, as well as two rest periods. At midday everyone breaks for lunch and a daily cleaning period to tidy up the school.

Hirofumi is in the sixth grade. He has the same teacher he had last year, Hamana-sensei. Masayo is in fourth grade. Her teacher is Harada-sensei. For special classes, students have other teachers.

Hirofumi's Japanese language textbook.

Masayo's language textbook.

Hirofumi and his class learn to play the recorder.

This morning Hirofumi begins with music class. All students learn to play an instrument, usually the recorder. In second period, they study the Japanese language. It takes years to learn how to read and write Japanese because it is made of two different alphabets. One, called *kanji*, has thousands of characters. Each symbolizes an object or idea. The other, called *kana*, has letters which represent sounds. It is more like the system we use to write English.

Today, Hamana-sensei divides the class into teams. Members of each team go to the blackboard and write the kanji for a word the teacher calls out. They often look up characters in their dictionaries.

Today in Masayo's second-period science class, her teacher, Harada-sensei, talks about the reproduction and growth of potatoes. Everyone grows a potato plant to study.

Above: Masayo eagerly responds to a question. Below: Hirofumi's class watches a history program.

Playing at School

After a break, Hirofumi has his social studies class. Today, there is a special program on TV about a Japanese emperor and empress and their royal family and palace hundreds of years ago. Many buildings in Japan were destroyed during World War II, but some palaces still stand in Kyoto and Nara, the old capitals of Japan.

Next Hirofumi goes to math class, which he likes. Everyone must do homework because Hamana-sensei will often ask students to come to the blackboard to test their math skills. Many students use their calculators, and some still use the abacus. This is an ancient instrument used for calculating which is made of beads on rods. Students must practice in order to use the abacus well.

Gym clothes hang in bags outside the classroom.

Special uniforms for gym class.

Ping-Pong is one of the school's club activities. Hirofumi is the captain of the Ping-Pong club.

At lunchtime everyone eats in their classroom. The school provides the lunch. Today it is curried rice and a bottle of milk. After lunch is recess. During break time everyone goes outside to let off some steam.

Sixth period changes daily. It is a time used for student committee meetings and teachers' projects. On Fridays, sixth period is used for club meetings. Every student belongs to a club of some kind. They have quite a few activities to choose from, including cooking, music, arts and crafts, cartoon drawing, Japanese chess, or *shogi*, and even a club that studies traditional children's games.

There are many sports clubs as well. Hirofumi and Masayo belong to the Ping-Pong club. Masayo is the only girl, but she loves Ping-Pong, so she doesn't mind. Students wear the same uniform for their sports club that they wear for gym class.

A clean, quiet lunchroom.

Students take turns serving one another.

Working at School

Everyone is expected to help keep the school clean. Students and teachers take off their shoes when they go inside, just as they do at home. There is a special shoe compartment for every student.

When inside the school, everyone wears special indoor shoes that help keep the floors clean. When they go outside they put their indoor shoes in a special compartment and change to their outdoor shoes. It may seem confusing, but Japanese children are used to it.

At lunchtime different students are assigned each day to help serve the food. Today it is Masayo's turn. She and the other servers first change into a special white uniform. She looks almost like a real chef in her white hat. After getting the food from the kitchen, they serve everyone in their class.

No food stains on these white uniforms!

Every day after recess there's a 20-minute cleaning time called *osoji*. All students are expected to do some cleaning chore around the school. In this way they show respect for their school. They also learn how to be neat.

Of course, being regular kids, some of the students don't think the cleaning period is fun. The boys, in particular, like to grumble as they sweep, dust, and scrub. Sometimes they get into water fights. So then the teacher reminds them why they are doing this. Many children live in small homes and share bedrooms with their brothers and sisters. In some homes the living room becomes the bedroom at night. So it's important that students learn to pick up any mess they make and to respect their home and school.

Masayo's class washes down the infirmary.

Hirofumi's class cleans the stairwells.

Above: Hirofumi's class and Hamana-sensei. Below: Masayo's class and Harada-sensei.

Respect for Elders

Children are taught to respect older people. Even adults pay respect to their elders. They believe that as persons age, they become wiser. So everyone listens to elders.

Students treat teachers with great respect. Students do not speak during class unless called on. They raise their hands and patiently wait their turn. In some schools, students stand by the desk before answering.

On trains, younger people give up their seats to older people, especially to those who have some injury. They help older people by opening doors or carrying their groceries. Masayo and Hirofumi always treat their grandparents with respect and do whatever they ask. People also respect their ancestors. The Japanese believe that even dead elders pass on wisdom. So they maintain ancestors' grave sites and say prayers for them. Grandmother Tanaka often prays at her home altar for her ancestors' peace in the afterlife.

Masayo and a friend practice on their recorders on the way home, while a third friend giggles at their performance.

Bowing in respect at the end of the day.

Donning outside shoes before going home.

What kind of water creature is this?

Masayo practices for her swimming teacher.

Hirofumi practices his backstroke.

Learning outside of School

On Sunday, there is no school, but the children still have lessons — they are off to swimming school. Hirofumi started swimming when he was eleven. Now he is confident about his crawl and backstroke. Masayo began lessons when she was nine and still needs work on her crawl, but she's an excellent kicker.

On weekdays, Hirofumi and Masayo also attend a *juku*, or evening school. After their school day, they have a few hours' break and then leave for juku, where they get individual attention with their studies. Competition to get into universities is intense. Students must pass a difficult entrance exam. Juku help them prepare for the exam by allowing them to work on weaker subjects. Once juku were only for high school students, but now children who are two or three attend.

Hirofumi likes the individual attention he gets.

Masayo attacks a math problem.

The children began at Nerima Juku when they were nine. Both study math, and Masayo also studies Japanese. At the age of five, they began attending an English juku.

The children have little free time. Some days, Hirofumi goes to juku until 10 p.m. but he doesn't mind. He thinks one or two hours of play a day are enough. At regular school he works in a group and helps others; at juku, he can learn at his own pace.

Sweets: dango, taiko yaki, and oranges.

Cooperation in the kitchen.

A Typical Evening Meal

For dinner tonight, Mother and Grandmother Funato prepare fish tempura. The fish is dipped into a small bowl of soy sauce, or *shoyu*, and grated radish, or *daikon*. Mother also makes a dish called *gomae* — green beans mixed with sesame seeds. She also serves a pickle salad with dressing, and a bowl of white rice. Father and Grandfather Funato drink beer while everyone else drinks green tea.

The family may eat their meal with chopsticks, called *ohashi*, or with knives, forks, and spoons.

Usually the family has fruit or ice cream for dessert. But sometimes Grandmother Funato will make some special treats. One, called *dango*, is pounded rice rolled into sticky balls and then dipped in a bittersweet sauce or covered in sweet, dark bean paste. Another treat is *taiko yaki*, a pancakelike pastry filled with the same sweet, dark bean paste. One fruit the family enjoys is mandarin oranges. They are like tangerines, only a bit sweeter and juicier.

Grandmother, Tsuta Tanaka, and grandfather, Kiichi Tanaka, at the family grave site.

Family Traditions

Families go three times a year to family graves. On these visits, called *ohigan*, they clean the grave site and pray for their ancestors' souls.

The Funatos follow Buddhist beliefs and worship at a temple, called *kougenji*. Every morning Grandmother Funato kneels before her shrine and prays for her family.

The shrine, or *butsudan*.

Yoshindo adjusts a computer.

A million people a day pass through some stations.

Work and Commuting

Yoshindo, an engineer, commutes one hour each way to work. This is typical in Tokyo, and trains are crowded during rush hour.

Kayoko clerks in a bank. She has been saving her salary for the children's university education. Schooling is expensive in Japan so families must begin saving when the children are still young.

The Neighborhood Shopping District

Grandmother Funato makes valuable contributions to the family. She is in charge of the house during the day, helps with the cleaning, and assists in making meals. She also does the shopping. Hirofumi and Masayo help her shop after school or on Sundays.

In Japan there are some large grocery stores, but most people still shop in the traditional manner. They go to their local shopping district where various stalls are set up outside smaller shops. It's something like a marketplace.

Here Grandmother Funato can buy vegetables from one vendor, tea from another, and a new cooking pot from another. She can give Hirofumi and Masayo some money to pick out fruit for dessert while she visits with her neighbors at the dairy stand.

The family shops every day because they don't have much room to store food. It's easier to pick up just enough for the day's meals. Grandmother Funato walks to the nearby shopping district, toting her shopping bag to carry home her groceries.

Because Japan is surrounded by oceans, seafood is plentiful, so people eat more seafood than meat. Cows and sheep need land to graze on, and land is precious on these islands. So there is little beef or mutton, and these meats are costly. Chicken is less expensive because it can be raised on much less land than the larger animals.

Narrow but clean streets in the Nerima shopping district. Many people use bicycles to travel through Tokyo, so the streets are lined with stalls for parking them.

Colorful displays.

The comic-book stand.

The mat maker repairs tatami mats.

The shopping district isn't just for food. Hirofumi looks through the toy stores for computer games. Every few weeks, a new game comes out. The shopkeeper knows Hirofumi well, and tells him when a new game arrives.

Nearby, in the magazine shop, Masayo buys comic books. She likes to know when a new episode of her favorite reading, *The Glass Mask*, comes out. She also looks for fashion magazines, to keep up with the latest trends. Hirofumi, too, likes to look through the magazines, especially the ones about computers and sports. Both children like to read. In fact, because of Japan's school system, about 99% of the people can read and write.

The tatami mat maker works just across the street from the Funatos' house. Because some Japanese are using Western furniture, there are fewer and fewer mat makers. The best mats are made by hand with great care taken to do delicate stitching and weaving.

Important stop! The sweet shop.

Masayo snacks on sushi.

All kinds of radishes.

Nutritious tofu is popular outside Japan, too.

Masayo buys tofu and radishes today. An inexpensive source of protein, tofu is made from soybeans and sold in blocks that look somewhat like cream cheese. Versatile cooks fry it, cut it up in salads, or even whip it to make a tofu shake. The tart radishes provide flavor and color in meals.

Kentucky Fried Chicken in Tokyo.

Another Japanese specialty is sushi, rice rolled in seaweed that can contain eggs, vegetables, and even raw fish. The Japanese buy this from stands, as we buy hot dogs. Of course, there is some Western food too. McDonald's, Burger King, and Kentucky Fried Chicken stands are found all over Tokyo. The hamburgers are expensive, but popular.

The trip takes forever but, at last, they arrive.

Below: A Disneyland palace.

The Tokyo Disneyland

They're off! A day at the Tokyo Disneyland. Many rides are the same as those in the United States. The boys run to the fast ones — particularly Space Mountain.

Mickey Mouse is the same the world over.

The girls like chills down the spine. They choose the Haunted Mansion. And, of course, they buy ice cream.

Disneyland is always crowded. Waiting to ride for an hour or more is not unusual. But the children don't mind as long as they have friends along to chatter with. It's just fun to have a day off to relax.

Opposite: Main Street, U.S.A. at the Tokyo Disneyland.

39

The students do warm-up exercises before the races begin.

Bewildered runners in a daruma race.

Everyone lines up as they do at school.

Sports Day

On *Undokai*, Sports Day, schools compete and parents watch. They have the usual track events. But some events are a little silly. The *daruma* race is a relay race in which runners can't see because they are wearing *papier-mâché* heads with no holes to see through. Led by a teammate, they must stumble to another teammate who, in turn, puts on the head and continues the race. All the while, the leader carries a ball in a scoop. If the ball drops as runners bumble about, they must start the race over!

In another contest, students make a pyramid. The top one wears a kabuto helmet that the other team tries to knock off.

Masayo sprints toward the finish line.

The pyramid game tumbles players about.

Fireworks at Tashimaen are popular.

So much to buy.

Fast rides and bright lights.

Kingyo sukui — a game of chance.

The Park and Cherry Blossom Time

In summer, the children visit Tashimaen Amusement Park. They like rides so much that they are happy for hours. For a break, they play games of chance. They lose a lot, but they have fun trying.

In spring, Japan celebrates the blooming of cherry trees. This is also a good time for games. Hirofumi tries the goldfish scoop game, *kingyo sukui*. The wriggly goldfish slip out of the scoop. Masayo buys a paper triangle. If a number appears inside, she selects a prize.

The Otori Sama Festival

In November, there is an *Otori Sama* festival. Otori Sama is the Japanese spirit of good fortune, money, and other riches. Hirofumi and Masayo can buy good-luck charms on this day, so they browse through the stalls, trying to find just the right one.

Masayo likes festival days for another reason. For a couple of years, she has been collecting mementos from her excursions in and around Tokyo. She is eager to look for something special that will remind her of the Otori Sama festival. This memento will go with the others that are already on her bookshelf. Someday soon, she thinks, she will need to weed out her mementos or ask her parents for more bookshelves.

Buying charms at the Otori Sama festival.

Pinball — a popular game of chance.

Masayo tries for a picture of her favorite singer.

A feast of colors and flavors awaits the family.

New Year's Day

New Year's Day is very important in Japan. Throughout the month of December, everyone works especially hard because it is traditional to pay off all debts by December 31. It is also important to thank business clients, neighbors, and friends for their help and kindness throughout the year. Then on New Year's Day everyone begins the year with a clean slate.

Each person has a hot towel, called *oshibori*, next to the plate for cleansing their hands.

The family celebrates the New Year with a feast of traditional foods. These foods must not only taste good, but look good too, for the Japanese people believe that beautiful food aids digestion.

Around the chopsticks is a paper showing the Chinese character koto buki, which represents longevity and good fortune. Everyone talks happily at mealtime, remembering the past and discussing the future.

Wrapping the long sash, or *obi*.

Setting off for the Shinto shrine.

White socks called *tabi* have a special slit between the toes for the sandal strap.

On New Year's Day, the family goes to the neighborhood Shinto shrine. Shintoism is an ancient religion that still plays a part in people's daily lives. Masayo agrees to don the traditional kimono, made of hand-woven silks and gold threads.

Everyone from the neighborhood is there. They throw coins into a wooden box near the shrine, pull on the colorful bell tassels, and clap hands twice. Then they pray for happiness in the coming year.

Each New Year, the family offers prayers called *hatsumode* at the Shinto shrine.

The skyscrapers of Shinjuku, a busy section of Tokyo, in the early hours of the morning.

FOR YOUR INFORMATION: Japan

Official Name: Nihon (or Nippon)
(nih-HONE)
("Land of the Rising Sun")

Capital: Tokyo

History

Descendants of the Sun Goddess

In ancient times, various tribes migrated from eastern Asia to the islands of Japan. There, they clashed with the Ainu, who lived on the islands, forcing them to move northward to the island of Hokkaido. In the 4th century AD, on the island of Honshu, rulers of one family became more powerful than those of other tribes. They claimed they were descended from the sun goddess Amaterasu, a deity worshipped in the Shinto religion which the tribes followed. All of Japan's emperors descended from these rulers, so a belief in their divinity remained in Japan until the end of World War II. With the help of warriors, the rulers became more and more powerful.

A Central Government Emerges

At this time, Japan borrowed ideas from China — writing and art, the teachings of Buddha and Confucius, and ideas about government. Following the Chinese, the Japanese replaced tribal chiefs with an emperor; he owned all land and collected taxes. For two centuries, nobles controlled the nation. The Fujiwaras, the most powerful of this group, still influence Japanese affairs through their descendants.

Knights and Lords

In the 12th century, certain events undermined the emperor's control: governmental corruption and the rise of nobles who took as much land as they could, built huge castles, and ruled separate domains. To protect their land and power, these lords, or *daimyo*, relied upon professional warriors called *samurai*, who were, in a way, like medieval knights. By the late 12th century, two samurai groups, the Taira and the Minamoto, dominated. The Minamotos revolted, and Yoritomo Minamoto became *shogun*, or military governor. Shoguns ran Japan for the next 700 years.

The First Europeans

In 1543, Portuguese traders visited Japan, followed by traders from Spain, England, and the Netherlands and, in 1549, by Francis Xavier, a Jesuit missionary. Hoping to attract trade, the government encouraged many Japanese to become Christians. Japan's leaders then began to fear that the missionaries would try to divide and conquer Japan. In 1587, leader Hideyoshi Toyotomi expelled missionaries from the country. When the Tokugawa shoguns came to power in 1603, they began to isolate Japan even more from the West. By 1636, a law decreed that no Japanese could leave the country and none then abroad could return. In 1639 Christianity was banned, converts persecuted, and foreigners barred from the country. Only a few Dutch and Chinese traders remained.

Seclusion and Unification

Emperors became mere figureheads and the Tokugawa shoguns reigned until 1867, controlling the samurai and the daimyo. They put the samurai into government, required the daimyo to spend six months in the capital, and prevented the daimyo from revolting by holding their families hostage in the capital when the daimyo returned home for six months to oversee their castles and land.

Market towns attracting artisans and merchants grew up around the castles of the daimyo, and a new class of people, merchants, became influential. They bought and sold the goods of artisans and farmers. But the samurai and daimyo despised the merchants. So, cut off from aristocratic culture, merchants sought their own. One art they supported was the *Kabuki* drama. Soon, a healthy economy and discontent among the peasants would set the stage for the end of isolation.

The End of Isolation

In 1854, Commodore Matthew Perry, who had arrived in Japan in 1853 with four US Navy ships, persuaded leaders to open the country to foreign trade. The long period of seclusion ended. The shogun signed treaties with the United States, Great Britain, Russia, Holland, and France, treaties that many Japanese considered unfair. They forced the shogun to resign, and in 1868, Emperor Mutsuhito, later called Meiji, regained the power former emperors had lost to the Tokugawa shoguns.

This began the period called the Meiji Restoration; it lasted until 1912. Meiji eliminated the rigid class system and encouraged industry and commerce under the management of the *zaibatsu*, large family corporations such as Mitsubishi and Mitsui, which are still among Japan's leading business organizations. In less than fifty years, Japan became a modern nation. It also became a military power.

Military Might

During the late 19th century and the early 20th century, Japan aggressively began acquiring land, coming into conflict with China and Russia. During World War I, Japan fought with Great Britain against Germany, and after the war put its energies into making changes at home rather than invading other nations. But the Great Depression of the 1930s increasingly drove people to seek military solutions to problems. The zaibatsu, who controlled the economy, began working with military leaders. Emperor Hirohito and elected officials had little power.

By 1940, Japan had invaded China, allied itself with Germany and Italy, who were fighting in Europe, and begun occupying French Indochina. The United States and Great Britain immediately stopped trading with Japan, and on December 7, 1941, the Japanese bombed the Philippines, Hong Kong, Malaya, and Pearl Harbor, in Hawaii. The United States declared war. At first successful, the Japanese began suffering defeat: a loss to the US Navy at Midway Island, in the Pacific, a shipping industry that was crippled, and the end of manufacturing in the cities undergoing bombing by the United States and its allies, which included Great Britain, France, and China. On August 6 and 9, 1945, the US dropped atomic bombs on Hiroshima and Nagasaki, and on August 8, another US ally, the Soviet Union, declared war. In August 1945, Emperor Hirohito demanded that the army surrender.

After the War

Allied military forces, under US General Douglas MacArthur, occupied Japan for seven years, hoping to aid Japan in establishing a democracy. During this time, Hirohito renounced his divine status, and wartime leaders, including the prime minister, General Hideki Tojo, were convicted of war crimes and executed. The Diet, or parliament, ratified a new constitution under which both houses were elected by the people; women were given equal voting rights, the right to own property, and the right to divorce; and the nation renounced war, although it will defend itself if attacked. Occupation forces withdrew in 1952 after Japan signed the San Francisco Peace Treaty, and in 1956 Japan joined the United Nations.

Since then, the nation's focus has been on rebuilding industry; it is now a leader in production of cars, steel, and electronic equipment, and builds more ships than any other nation. Increasingly, it has cut its ties to the United States and has taken an independent and active role in world affairs. Emperor Hirohito died in January 1989 and was succeeded by his son, Akihito. Although World War II veterans' groups in the United States protested, the United States joined over 160 governments worldwide in sending representatives to his state funeral in February 1989.

Government

Today, Japan is a constitutional monarchy with a parliamentary system of government. The emperor is the symbolic leader of the nation but has little power. The head of the government is actually the prime minister, the leader of the majority party in the Diet. The emperor officially chooses the prime minister, but in reality, he only approves the choice of the Diet.

The prime minister heads the executive branch and appoints his cabinet, which is responsible for administering the various agencies of the government. The agencies deal with matters such as technology, science, economic planning, and national defense. The Diet, the legislative branch, has two divisions, both elected by the people: the House of Councillors and the House of Representatives. A bill passed by both houses becomes law, as does a bill approved by two-thirds of the representatives, even if the councillors veto it.

A Supreme Court consisting of a chief justice and 14 other justices heads the judicial branch. The cabinet appoints judges for ten-year terms; voters approve these appointments every term. Japan also has district courts, summary courts, family courts, and high courts, which hear criminal and civil appeals.

Citizens may vote at age 20. The Liberal-Democratic party (LDP) has been in power since the 1950s. But in 1989, scandal shook the LDP when top officials were accused of accepting improper stock offers. Prime Minister Noboru Takeshita resigned, and his successor, Sosuke Uno, has been accused of immorality and forced to resign. Many people are wondering if the LDP can recover public confidence.

The chief opposition party is the Socialist party, which controls fewer than one-fourth of the seats in the two houses. Two small but vocal parties represent more extreme views: the Communist party and the Komeito, or Clean Government, party, which has Buddhist ties.

Religion

The early tribes of Japan worshipped gods who controlled objects or forces of nature, such as the moon, the stars, rivers, and even some animals and vegetables. These beliefs and rituals were the basis of the Shinto religion, which still emphasizes an attitude of reverence for nature.

Shinto became the state religion in the late 19th century. But military men in government tried to use it to persuade people to accept their policies, so after World War II, the state withdrew support for Shintoism and a new constitution gave the Japanese religious freedom.

In Asakusa, worshipers carry a portable shrine called *omikoshi* during the yearly Sanja Matsuri festival.

In the 6th century AD, Japan learned about Buddhism. About 75% of the people are Buddhists, but they do not worship as Westerners do. They do not go to a temple each week, for instance, but live with the teachings of Buddha as part of their daily lives. Many also retain Shinto beliefs. A family may have both a Buddhist altar at which they honor ancestors and a Shinto shrine devoted to the gods. Devout families might begin the day with the Buddhist ceremony of burning incense in honor of the dead and clap their hands in tribute to the Shinto gods. They could perform both Buddhist rites at funerals and Shinto rituals at births and marriages.

Confucianism, a philosophy rather than a religion, appeared in the 4th century AD. Many of the ethical teachings of Confucius influence Japanese religion. Complete obedience to a father or lord is one principle that guided the samurai warriors.

At first missionaries like Francis Xavier were successful in spreading Christianity, but the religion was banned in the 17th century when foreigners were expelled from the country. Today, less than one percent of the population is Christian.

Population and Ethnic Groups

Japan has nearly 125 million people, with a density of almost 813 people per square mile (314 per sq km). Over 75% of the people live in urban areas. The largest minority group in Japan is composed of 660 thousand Koreans, who have their own culture and speak Korean. The number of Caucasians and Chinese is much smaller. Most of the people of Japan share a common language and culture.

Two tribal ethnic groups remain. The Ainu are descended from the islands' original inhabitants and, until recently, lived in reed houses, wore bark clothing, and spoke a unique language. They have adopted modern culture recently and are barely a separate ethnic group. The Buramkumin are descended from social outcasts who lived by slaughtering animals, tanning hides, and working in leather — undesirable jobs to most Japanese. They still fill the lowest-paid jobs. Though equal by law since 1868, they are discriminated against in education and employment. They live in segregated communities and do not marry outside their own group.

Education

The Japanese value education and 99% of the people can read and write. Everyone between the ages of six and fifteen must go to school. Students spend six years in elementary school and three in junior high school. More than 90% of the students continue their education after age fifteen even though it is no longer compulsory and even though public as well as private senior high schools charge tuition. Senior high schools provide three years of technical training or college preparatory classes and all teach English.

About one-third of the high school graduates go on to a university, junior college, or advanced technical school. To prepare for entrance examinations, many attend juku, or "extra-hour," schools. Because major universities have waiting lists, even students who do well on entrance exams may have to wait six years to get in.

Language

Japanese is a complicated written language, combining two different methods of putting spoken language on paper. One part of the language consists of kanji, which are ideographs, or picture symbols. These stand for whole words or ideas, like "flower" or "friend." Over 1,500 years ago, the Japanese borrowed the kanji from the Chinese.

Then the Japanese developed other characters, called kana, which stand for sounds. Most writing is now a combination of kanji and kana. There were once thousands of kanji characters. But after World War II, the government reduced the number and simplified the forms. Still, the people have to learn at least 1,850 kanji characters in order to read their books and magazines.

Spoken Japanese has some resemblance to the Korean language. Kanto, the dialect spoken in Tokyo, is the standard form of spoken Japanese, but many people also speak the dialect of the region in which they live. As with the different dialects of English, sometimes people who speak one dialect of Japanese cannot understand people from other parts of the country.

Land and Climate

An ancient temple hidden in the autumn forest.

Japan is a narrow ribbon of over 3,000 islands in the western Pacific Ocean. The four largest islands of Honshu, Hokkaido, Kyushu, and Shikoku account for 98% of the area. The islands making up the other 2% are much smaller and often uninhabited. Japan is slightly smaller than Newfoundland or California, with a total area of about 146,000 square miles (378,000 sq km); its shape is long and narrow. Its total length is about 1,880 miles (3,030 km), which is about the distance from the southern border of California to the northern tip of Vancouver Island.

The open waters of the Pacific stretch to the east and south of Japan's four large islands. To the west and north are the East China Sea, the Sea of Japan, and the Sea of Okhotsk, arms of the Pacific separating Japan from the USSR and Asia.

The islands of Japan are actually the tops of an undersea mountain range rising from the floor of the ocean. This is why only 20% of the surface area of Japan is level. Short, swift streams flow through steep-sided valleys in the mountains and deposit sediment and gravel on the plains along the coast. These coastal plains are the sites of Japan's largest cities. Heavy rains, especially in the typhoon season, often cause severe flooding and destruction of property in these areas.

Every year there are more than 1,500 earth tremors in Japan; earthquakes strong enough to damage buildings occur every five or six years. Undersea earthquakes can produce a tsunami, or giant tidal wave. In 1923, 200 thousand people lost their lives in the Great Kanto Earthquake. The quake and the tsunami that swept over the plain destroyed much of Tokyo and almost all of Yokohama.

There are about 200 volcanoes in the mountains of Japan; about 50% are active. Mount Fuji, Japan's highest mountain, is a volcano that has not erupted since 1707. Hot springs surround the active volcanoes and when one erupts, hot water may spurt from the ground and flow into the mountain streams.

Japan has a moderate climate. In the north, temperatures average 22°F (-6°C) in the winter and 68°F (20°C) in the summer. In the south, they average 60°F (16°C) in the winter and 83°F (28°C) in the summer. In winter, cold winds out of Siberia bring deep snows to the north. In late summer and early fall, typhoons may batter the islands with raging winds and torrential rains. Normal rainfall varies quite a bit by area: rainfall averages 33 inches (84 cm) in eastern Hokkaido, 62 inches (158 cm) in Tokyo, and 150 inches (380 cm) in central Honshu.

54

Agriculture

Only 20% of the land in Japan is flat enough to be farmed, and the soil is not naturally fertile. Farmers have increased farmland by terracing mountain slopes. They have fertilized soil, until today an acre has one of the highest yields in the world. The warm south produces two crops a year. Mandarin oranges are a major crop but rice is Japan's largest crop, and paddies make up half the cultivated land. But despite all this, about 30% of Japan's food must still be imported. Market gardens encircling major cities provide fresh vegetables to the urban areas.

Japanese farms are small, averaging about three acres (1.2 ha). Japanese farm life is changing. Many farmers now work in the cities and return to their farms only on weekends. Older members of the family and school-age children do much of the actual farm work.

Natural Resources

Japan leads the world in the tonnage of fish caught commercially. Its large, modern fleets usually include a mother ship, a plant where the fish are processed and canned while the ship is at sea. The ships of Japan's whaling fleet are also factory ships that completely process whales without having to return to shore.

Japan is a member of the International Whaling Commission, which protects whales of endangered species but, in spite of this, Japan has been accused of overhunting them and threatening their survival. In recent years, the Japanese have begun to practice "sea farming." In the shallow bays along the coast, they plant beds of prawns, oysters, and edible seaweed.

Much of Japan's timber is in the mountains and difficult to reach with the machinery necessary for commercial cutting. In the past, mountain villagers cut the trees by hand and made charcoal from the wood. Gas and electricity have replaced charcoal as a household fuel but there is a need for wood pulp and wood products. Japan imports over half its wood from Indonesia and the Philippines.

Industry

Industry has grown enormously since World War II, although bombs destroyed many factories then, and Japan is not rich in natural resources. It imports many essentials for manufacturing, including iron ore, coal, and great amounts of oil.

The economy is heavily dependent upon giant organizations called zaibatsu, which have existed since the late 19th century, when the country first became an industrial nation. Under the zaibatsu, Japan has become the world's leading producer of television sets, ships, and pianos. It ranks second in the manufacture of cars, synthetic textiles, and radios, and third in the production of steel.

JAPAN — Political and Physical

HEIGHT IN FEET AND METERS

feet	meters	
12,000	4,000	
6,000	2,000	
3,000	1,000	
1,000	300	Above Sea Level
0	0	Sea Level

0   100   200   300   km

0   100   200 miles

PACIFIC OCEAN

Sea of Okhotsk

SEA   OF   JAPAN

USSR

CHINA

NORTH KOREA

P'yongyang

SOUTH KOREA

Seoul

Oki Islands

HOKKAIDO

Point Soya

Yubetsu

Kitami

Shari

L.
Kutcharo

Teshio

Ishikari

Shiribetsu

Tokachi

Sapporo

Ishikari Bay

Uchiura Bay

Tsugaru Strait

Cape Erimo

JAPAN

HONSHU

Iwate
6,698 ft/2,041 m

Towada

Oshi

Kitakami

Abukuma

Mogami

Inahashiro

Tone

Naka

Hitachi

Cape Inubo

Boso
Peninsula

Tokyo

Yokohama

Kyo Bay

Cape Nojima

Fuji
12,389 ft/3,776 m

Fuji

Gifu

Iida

Ono

Komatsu

Kanazawa

Wakasa Bay

Kiso

Chikuma

Point Suzu

Noto
Peninsula

Toyama Bay

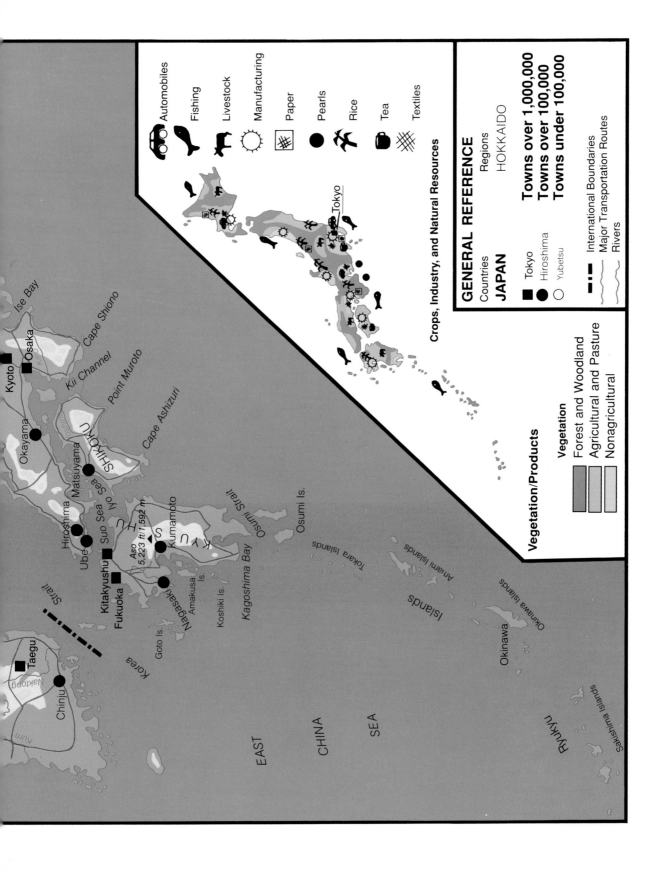

GENERAL REFERENCE

Countries   Regions
JAPAN   HOKKAIDO

Tokyo   ■   Towns over 1,000,000
Hiroshima ●   Towns over 100,000
Yubetsu   ○   Towns under 100,000

           International Boundaries
           Major Transportation Routes
           Rivers

Vegetation/Products

Vegetation

Forest and Woodland
Agricultural and Pasture
Nonagricultural

Crops, Industry, and Natural Resources

Automobiles
Fishing
Livestock
Manufacturing
Paper
Pearls
Rice
Tea
Textiles

Tokyo

Ise Bay
Kyoto
Osaka
Cape Shiono
Kii Channel
Point Muroto
Cape Ashizuri
Okayama
SHIKOKU
Matsuyama
Hiroshima
Iyo Sea
Suo Sea
Ube
Kitakyushu
Fukuoka
Aso 5,223 ft/1,592 m
Kumamoto
Nagasaki
Amakusa Is.
Koshiki Is.
Kagoshima Bay
Osumi Strait
Osumi Is.
Tokara Islands
Amami Islands
Islands
Okinawa Islands
Okinawa
Ryukyu
Sakishima Islands

Strait
Taegu
Naktong
Chinju
Kŭm
Korea

EAST
CHINA
SEA

Typical Japanese workers stay with the same employer all their working life. In recent years, however, there has been a change in the relative proportion of workers in various occupations. Over half the people work in business or service industries, 25% in manufacturing, 9% in construction, 9% in agriculture and fishing, and 3% in government and public service.

The Arts

Drama

Japanese drama of the past remains popular today. TV programs include revered *Noh*, *Bunraku*, and Kabuki plays. Noh plays, first performed in the 14th century, combine poetry, chants, drums and flutes, and slow, formal dancing. Their stories about gods, warriors, and heroic deeds often have a tragic ending. The cast has two important characters and a chorus. The actors, all men, wear painted masks.

The Bunraku puppet plays appeared in the 17th century. They combine dialogue with dancing and music played on the *samisen*, an instrument shaped like a banjo. Bunraku plays are serious but dramatize the lives of ordinary people. The puppets of the Bunraku theater are about half life-size and are moved about by three men who never speak but are visible to the audience. They coordinate the puppets' movements with the chanted dialogue and description of a narrator who stands at the side of the stage.

Wealthy merchants supported Kabuki drama; they are less formal than the Noh plays and have lots of physical action. Some action takes place on a runway that runs from the back of the theater to the stage. Dogs, horses, and demons appear among the characters. Actors play a variety of roles and start training in childhood to perfect their voices, their dancing, and their acrobatic skills. The actors may wear costumes weighing as much as 50 pounds (23 kg), and some paint their faces in white, black, and red. Besides these traditional plays, Japanese theatergoers can see other plays — from Shakespeare to modern works popular in North America.

Literature

Japan holds a yearly poetry contest, and at New Year's the emperor awards a prize for the best. Most poems are written in traditional patterns used for centuries, like the *haiku*, a three-line poem with a specific number of syllables but no rhyme. Because the poem is so short, there is room for only a few descriptive details.

In the early 11th century, a noblewoman of the court wrote *The Tale of Genji*. The name she wrote under was Shikibu Murasaki, but her real name has never been known. Her story, the adventures of Prince Genji, was the first novel written in any language, and people still enjoy it. Many modern Japanese novelists write another kind of book which they call the "I novel" because it is based on the writer's own life and experiences.

Painting

Traditional Japanese paintings are like haiku poems. The artist uses only a few brush strokes to suggest the details of the scene. The details are realistic but the painting is not like a photograph, because the artist chooses only certain details. Japanese painters have used the same technique to decorate fans, sliding doors, and screens with landscapes and scenes from nature.

Early artists painted scrolls that were held in the hands and then unrolled to reveal different parts of a picture that often reached a length of as much as 30 feet (9 m). Many painters were also calligraphers and used hand lettering in their designs as well as lettering and illustrating scrolls containing poems, diaries, and stories.

Sports

The Japanese enjoy traditional sports as much as they do traditional drama and art. *Sumo* is a Japanese form of wrestling; professional sumo wrestlers compete in national tournaments held every year. Samurai martial skills have become competitive sports in Japan. In a sport called *kendo*, players fence with bamboo poles. Judo, which developed from methods of self-defense, and karate, a dangerous martial art, are nearly as popular in other countries as they are in Japan.

The Japanese have enthusiastically adopted some of the sports of the West. Baseball is popular nationwide, and winter sports draw many to the cold mountains of the northern island of Hokkaido. Tokyo was host to the summer Olympic Games in 1964, and the winter Olympics of 1972 were held in Sapporo.

Tokyo

Edo, the unofficial seat of government for the Tokugawa shoguns, was renamed Tokyo in 1868, under Emperor Meiji. Tokyo is now the official capital and Japan's financial, commercial, and cultural center. Visitors flock to the city's museums and theaters, and tourists and worshippers come to see the Meiji Shrine.

Restaurants on the Kamogawa River, in Kyoto.

Tokyo, with Yokohama and Kawasaki, is part of what is known as the Greater Keihin Metropolitan Area; 25% of Japan's people live here. Tokyo alone covers 830 square miles (2,150 sq km) and contains over eight million people. Building has almost stopped in the city, where the population is dropping. Increasingly, people are moving to the suburbs. Tokyo's rapid growth has caused air pollution, waste disposal problems, and urban sprawl, urban problems everywhere.

The Keihin industrial region, which produces nearly 20% of the nation's goods by value, runs along Tokyo Bay, from Tokyo to Yokohama. A railroad system built during the Meiji period (1868-1912) brings lines into Tokyo from all over Japan. Some stations handle 400 thousand to nearly 2 million passengers a day. Now, people also use express railroads, called *shinkansen*.

The emperor and his family live in the Imperial Palace in the old town of Edo, in Tokyo. The palace and its surrounding park cover 250 acres (100 ha). Nearby are government buildings. In outer regions of the Keihin metropolitan area are shops, financial offices, hospitals, and over 100 universities.

High-rise buildings of 40 to 50 stories are now common; the Sunshine 60 building, completed in 1978, has 60 stories. Such heights are unusual, because Japan experiences more than 1,000 earth tremors each year and serious earthquakes every five or six years.

Currency

The unit of currency in Japan is the *yen*. As of late August 1989, 138 yen were equal to one United States dollar.

Japanese in North America

The different generations of Japanese descendants have specific labels. The immigrants are called *Issei*; the second generation, born in a new country, are *Nisei*; their children are *Sansei*. Japanese immigrants began arriving in North America in the 1880s. They settled on the West Coast. Today, Hawaii and California have large populations of US citizens of Japanese descent. During World War II, 110 thousand people of Japanese descent were forced from the West Coast to concentration camps further inland. Two-thirds were US citizens. They lost businesses, jobs, and homes; in 1988, the US government decided to pay them $20,000 each for their losses, but so far none of these people has received any money.

Japanese companies have moved to the southern United States, and investors are buying real estate in the East. Many Japanese come to North America as students and tourists; honeymooners particularly like Hawaii and San Francisco!

Glossary of Useful Japanese Terms

Bunraku (BOON-rah-koo) .... traditional puppet plays
daimyo (DIME-yoh) .... a great landowner or lord
haiku (HY-koo) .... three-line, 17-syllable poems
Issei (EE-say) .... Japanese immigrants to another nation
Kabuki (kah-BOO-kee) .... drama with exciting physical action
kana (KAH-nah) .... written characters that stand for sounds
kanji (KAN-jee) .... ideographs or picture symbols
for sounds
Nisei (NEE-say) .... children of Japanese immigrants
samurai (SAHM-oor-eye) .... a warrior-knight
Sansei (SAHN-say) .... grandchildren of Japanese immigrants

More Books About Japan

Count Your Way Through Japan. Haskins (Carolrhoda Books)
Japan. Crush (Silver Burdett)
Japan. Jacobsen (Childrens Press)
Japan: Where East Meets West. Davidson (Dillon)
The Japanese in America. Leathers (Lerner)
Samurai of Gold Hill. Uchida (Creative Arts)
A Year of Japanese Festivals. Epstein and Epstein (Garrard)

Things to Do — Research Projects

Japan places great emphasis on education, so parents, teachers, and students work toward the success of the student. Occasionally, the Japanese people worry about pressure on children, and the media are reporting more on this subject.

As you read about Japan or any country, keep in mind the importance of having up-to-date information. Some of the projects that follow require accurate, current information. Two publications your library may have will tell you about recent magazine and newspaper articles on many topics:

Readers' Guide to Periodical Literature
Children's Magazine Guide

1. Try to learn about one of the Japanese zaibatsu, or large corporations. Their names probably appear on many of the cars you see in your neighborhood every day as well as on some of the electronic equipment your family uses for cooking, cleaning, and entertainment.

2. Imagine what it might be like to be a daimyo or a samurai warrior. Investigate further into the lives of these people so important to Japan's history.

More Things to Do — Activities

1. Learn more about Buddhist religious days. With a group of friends or class-mates, plan a religious festival. Try to learn why this holiday is important to Buddhists, what foods they might serve, and what rituals they would perform.

2. One skill that the Japanese people enjoy is the art of *bonsai*, which comes from the Chinese words meaning "planting in a pan." When doing bonsai, one trains small plants to grow in certain ways and in certain directions. Check your library or bookstore to see how you would get started doing bonsai yourself. See if any of your local plant stores have bonsai plants that you could look at.

3. Another art in Japan is called origami. It is the art of paper folding. If you become good at origami, you will be able to create a bird or tree or house or even a monkey, just by folding paper. See if your library or bookstore has a book that will show you how to make your own origami creations.

4. If you would like a pen pal in Japan, write to these people:

International Pen Friends
P.O. Box 290065
Brooklyn, NY 11229

Worldwide Pen Friends
P.O. Box 39097
Downey, CA 90241

Be sure to tell them that you want your pen pal to be from Japan. Also include your name, address, and age.

Index